The Wonderful World of
Seals and Whales

by Sandra Lee Crow

A curious seal peeks into a diver's underwater camera.

BOOKS FOR YOUNG EXPLORERS
NATIONAL GEOGRAPHIC SOCIETY

Sea lions twist and do somersaults
in the water. One comes so close you can
see its whiskers. Sea lions are a kind of seal.

Seals paddle and steer with their strong flippers.
Their smooth bodies slip easily through the sea.
Blubber, the fat under their skin, helps keep seals warm.

Seals spend most of their lives in the water. But they come ashore to rest and to have their young. On a crowded beach, penguins waddle past resting seals and dark baby seals. Some baby seals have dark fur, while others have white fur. Baby seals are called pups. The pup drinks its mother's milk. Like a puppy dog, the seal is a mammal.

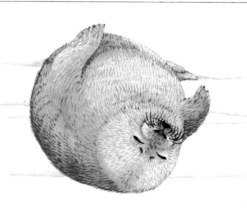

On rocky shores where seals gather, pups climb and play.
Different kinds of seals rest side by side. One pup sits on a neighbor,
a sleepy elephant seal. The fur seal pups all look alike.
How can a mother find her own? She barks, and the pup answers,
"Ma-a-a!" She sniffs it. She knows its sound and its smell.

A mother sea lion returns from eating fish in the sea. Two young sea lions come to meet her. Both call out to be fed.

The bigger pup may try to nurse, but it is old enough to find food on its own.

After playing by the water, a sea lion pup follows its mother up the beach to nurse. Sea lions and fur seals walk on all four flippers. Most other seals, such as harbor seals, use only their front flippers to move on land.

S eals often rest in groups.
These sea lions lie on rocks in the sun.
Soon they will dive into the sea.

Down by the water, a harbor seal
stretches to scratch its side with the
nails on its flipper. An elephant seal
flips cool, wet sand over its back.

When it is old enough, a seal finds its food
in the sea. This sea lion glides above a school of fish.

Riding a wave, another sea lion tosses a fish in the air.
Then it catches the fish in its mouth and swallows it whole.

Large eyes, opened wide, help a harp seal see beneath the ice. A seal pokes its head above water to breathe. Like all mammals, seals breathe air.

Flattening its body, a sea lion speeds through the water. What other mammals live in the sea?

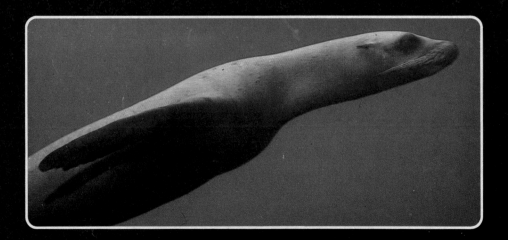

Walrus

mother

pup

Harp seal

Sea lion

Spinner dolphin

Humpback whale

Blue whale

Fur seal

female

male

Elephant seal

Killer whale

Harbor seal

Right whale

White whale

Whales large and small are swimming to and fro. Like seals, whales have flippers on their sides. Whale tails have fins called flukes. Flukes and flippers help whales swim. Unlike seals, whales spend their whole lives in the water.

whale breathes through a hole on top of its head.
At the surface of the water, it blows out old air and takes in
fresh air. This white whale has opened its blowhole to breathe.
It will close the blowhole when it dives under the water again.

As a whale breathes out, you can see its blow, or spray.
Some whales have two blowholes. Their spray makes a V.

A baby whale, which is called a calf, gets a piggyback ride from its mother. Born underwater, the calf must swim right away to the surface for its first breath. The calf drinks its mother's milk for about a year. Then it can find its own food in the sea.

A killer whale leaps into the air and crashes down with a splash. It is breaching.

A whale may poke its head above water and look around. This is called spy-hopping. Sometimes it slaps the water with its tail as it dives. No one knows exactly why whales do these things.

How do you think whales catch their food? Some, like the killer whale, grab fish with their big teeth and gulp them down.

Other whales strain their food from the sea with baleen. Baleen looks like a comb growing from the whale's top jaw.

Baleen whales eat krill, tiny sea animals that look like shrimp. Thousands of krill make a soup for these humpback whales.

A whale gulps water full of krill. Its throat bulges like a balloon. As the water goes out of the whale's mouth, the baleen catches the krill.

Playful dolphins jump
high in the air. They live
in a sea-life park.
These trained animals
are fun to watch.

Dolphins are small
whales. In parks and
aquariums, scientists
can study sea mammals
up close to learn
how they behave and
what they need.

A mother whale and her calf rest in the water. Scientists and their children study them quietly from a small boat.

We can watch seals when they come to shore. We may get a quick look at whales when they rise from their watery home. But there are still many mysteries about these mammals that live in the sea.

PUBLISHED BY The National Geographic Society
Gilbert M. Grosvenor, PRESIDENT
Melvin M. Payne, CHAIRMAN OF THE BOARD
Owen R. Anderson, EXECUTIVE VICE PRESIDENT
Robert L. Breeden, VICE PRESIDENT, PUBLICATIONS AND EDUCATIONAL MEDIA

PREPARED BY The Special Publications Division
Donald J. Crump, DIRECTOR
Philip B. Silcott, ASSOCIATE DIRECTOR
William L. Allen, ASSISTANT DIRECTOR

STAFF FOR THIS BOOK
Jane H. Buxton, MANAGING EDITOR
Thomas B. Powell III, PICTURE EDITOR
Cinda Rose, ART DIRECTOR
Peggy D. Winston, RESEARCHER
Tony Chen, CONTRIBUTING ARTIST
Carol Rocheleau Curtis, ILLUSTRATIONS ASSISTANT
Nancy F. Berry, Cricket Brazerol, Dianne T. Craven, Brenda J. Davis, Mary Elizabeth Davis, Rosamund Garner, Cleo Petroff,
Sheryl A. Prohovich, Nancy E. Simson, Pamela Black Townsend, Virginia A. Williams, STAFF ASSISTANTS

ENGRAVING, PRINTING, AND PRODUCT MANUFACTURE
Robert W. Messer, MANAGER
George V. White, PRODUCTION MANAGER
George J. Zeller, Jr., PRODUCTION PROJECT MANAGER
Mark R. Dunlevy, David V. Showers, Gregory Storer, ASSISTANT PRODUCTION MANAGERS
Mary A. Bennett, PRODUCTION ASSISTANT; Julia F. Warner, PRODUCTION STAFF ASSISTANT

CONSULTANTS
Lynda Ehrlich, READING CONSULTANT
Lila Bishop, EDUCATIONAL CONSULTANT
Thomas J. McIntyre, National Marine Fisheries Service/NOAA; Dr. Daryl J. Boness, National Zoological Park, SCIENTIFIC CONSULTANTS

ILLUSTRATIONS CREDITS
Akira Uchiyama (cover); David Doubilet (1, 2 inset, 2-3, 14-15); Jen and Des Bartlett (4, 6-7, 12, 21, 30-31); G.M. Wellington/University of Houston (5 left);
Tom J. Ulrich (5 right); Fred Bruemmer (6 upper left, 10-11, 13 lower, 32); Stephen J. Krasemann/DRK PHOTO (6 lower); Sullivan & Rogers/BRUCE COLEMAN INC. (8-9);
Robert C. Gildart (13 upper); Gregory Silber/WEST COAST WHALE RESEARCH FOUNDATION (15 upper); Bill Curtsinger (16-17); William R. Fraser (17 upper inset); Lewis
Trusty (17 lower inset); E.R. Degginger/BRUCE COLEMAN INC. (20); Flip Nicklin/NICKLIN & ASSOCIATES (22-23); Graeme Ellis/WEST COAST WHALE RESEARCH FOUNDATION
(24 upper left, 24-25); François Gohier (24 lower); M. Timothy O'Keefe (25 lower); Jen and Des Bartlett/BRUCE COLEMAN INC. (28-29).

Library of Congress CIP Data
Crow, Sandra Lee, 1948-
    The wonderful world of seals and whales.

    (Books for young explorers)
    Summary: Text and photographs present information about seals and whales.
    1. Seals—Juvenile literature. 2. Whales—Juvenile literature.
[1. Seals. 2. Whales] I. Title. II. Series.
QL737.P64C77 1984   599.74'5   84-14893
ISBN 0-87044-527-8 (regular edition)
ISBN 0-87044-532-4 (library edition)

Cover: A baby harp seal's coat is fluffy white.
Soon the pup will shed this coat and grow a
smoother, spotted one more like its mother's.
Below: Near a hole in the sea ice, a
mother harp seal sniffs her pup. Can you
find drawings of this pup in the book?